NOR...

Travel Guide

Contents

NORWAY

Introduction to Norway

Norway, a land of breathtaking landscapes, rich cultural heritage, and a history woven into the fabric of its fjords and mountains, invites travelers to embark on a remarkable journey. Situated in Northern Europe on the western part of the Scandinavian Peninsula, Norway is renowned for its natural beauty, encompassing fjords, glaciers, and lush greenery.

Geography: Norway's geographical splendor is characterized by its dramatic fjords, deep-blue lakes, and towering mountains. The country shares its eastern border with Sweden, while the North Sea lies to the southwest. Norway's northern regions extend beyond the Arctic Circle, treating visitors to the mesmerizing phenomenon of the Northern Lights.

History: Delving into Norway's history reveals a captivating tale of Viking sagas, medieval kingdoms, and modern prosperity. The Vikings, seafaring warriors from the late eighth to early 11th century, have left an indelible mark on Norwegian history. The country later saw the formation of a united kingdom in the 9th century and underwent various geopolitical changes before gaining independence in 1905.

Culture· Norwegian culture reflects a harmonious blend of ancient traditions and contemporary influences. The Norse mythology and folklore, including tales of trolls and mythical creatures, add a mystical touch to the cultural tapestry. The indigenous Sami people in the northern regions contribute to the diversity with their unique language and vibrant traditions.

Fun Facts:

1. Norway is home to the famous fjords, including the longest, Sognefjord, stretching over 200 kilometers.

2. The country boasts a remarkable 20,000 cabins, or "hytter," providing locals and tourists alike with cozy retreats in nature.

3. Norway consistently ranks high on global happiness indexes, with a strong emphasis on quality of life.

4. The midnight sun graces Norway's northern regions during the summer months, offering an enchanting natural spectacle.

5. Norwegian cuisine features traditional dishes like rakfisk (fermented fish) and lutefisk (dried fish reconstituted in a lye solution), showcasing the country's culinary diversity.

Embark on a captivating journey through Norway, where nature's wonders meet a rich cultural heritage, creating an unforgettable experience for every traveler.

Getting to Know Norwegian Cities

Norway's cities are vibrant hubs that seamlessly blend modernity with a deep-rooted connection to nature. Each city tells a unique story, inviting travelers to explore their cultural treasures and picturesque surroundings.

Oslo: The Capital City

Overview: Oslo, the capital and largest city of Norway, is a dynamic metropolis nestled between the Oslofjord and lush green hills. Boasting a mix of contemporary architecture and historical gems, Oslo is a cultural haven.

Attractions:

1. Vigeland Park: Home to over 200 sculptures by Gustav Vigeland, depicting the circle of life.
2. The Royal Palace: A majestic symbol of the Norwegian monarchy, surrounded by beautiful gardens.
3. The Viking Ship Museum: Showcasing well-preserved Viking ships and artifacts.

Unique Features:

• Oslo is a cyclist-friendly city with numerous biking trails, allowing visitors to explore at their own pace.
• The city's culinary scene offers a delightful fusion of traditional Nordic flavors and international influences.

Bergen: The Gateway to the Fjords

Overview: Known as the "Gateway to the Fjords," Bergen is a picturesque city surrounded by mountains and fjords. Its colorful wooden houses and rich maritime history make it a UNESCO World Heritage site.

Attractions:

1.Bryggen Wharf: Iconic colorful buildings housing shops, restaurants, and museums.

2.Fløibanen Funicular: A scenic ride to the top of Mount Fløyen for panoramic views of the city.

3.Fish Market: A bustling market offering fresh seafood and local delicacies.

Unique Features:

•Bergen experiences a high amount of rainfall, contributing to its lush surroundings and vibrant greenery.

•The annual Bergen International Festival attracts artists and performers from around the world.

Trondheim: The Historical Hub

<u>Overview:</u> Trondheim, with its rich medieval history and impressive architecture, stands as a testament to Norway's past. The Nidelva River winds through the city, adding to its charm.

<u>Attractions:</u>

1.Nidaros Cathedral: A stunning Gothic cathedral and Norway's national sanctuary.

2.Old Town Bridge: A historic bridge connecting the city center to the charming Bakklandet district.

3.Ringve Museum of Musical History: Showcasing a vast collection of musical instruments.

<u>Unique Features:</u>

•Trondheim is known for its cycling culture, with bike-friendly paths and bike-sharing initiatives.

•The city hosts the St. Olav Festival, celebrating its patron saint with music, art, and cultural events.

Stavanger: Coastal Beauty

Overview: Situated on the southwestern coast, Stavanger is a coastal gem surrounded by fjords and sandy beaches. Its modern vibe is complemented by a strong connection to the sea.

Attractions:

1.Preikestolen (Pulpit Rock): A breathtaking cliff offering panoramic views over Lysefjord.

2.Stavanger Cathedral: The city's oldest cathedral with a mix of Romanesque and Gothic architecture.

3.Norwegian Petroleum Museum: Detailing Norway's offshore oil and gas industry.

Unique Features:

•Stavanger's Old Town, Gamle Stavanger, features well-preserved wooden houses from the 18th century.

•The annual Gladmat Festival celebrates local and international culinary delights.

Norwegian Nature and Landscapes

Norway's unparalleled natural beauty is a symphony of fjords, mountains, waterfalls, and national parks. This chapter invites you to embark on a journey through the captivating landscapes that define the soul of Norway.

Fjords: Nature's Masterpiece

Norway's fjords are iconic wonders, carved by ancient glaciers and embraced by steep cliffs. The juxtaposition of serene waters and towering mountains creates a visual spectacle that leaves an indelible mark on every traveler.

Geirangerfjord:

Nestled amidst snow-capped peaks, Geirangerfjord is a UNESCO World Heritage site known for its mirror-like waters and cascading waterfalls, including the famous Seven Sisters.

Nærøyfjord:

A narrow and majestic fjord, Nærøyfjord boasts dramatic landscapes with lush greenery and pristine waters. It's a haven for kayakers and nature enthusiasts.

Mountains: Majestic Peaks and Hiking Trails

Norway's mountainous terrain offers not only breathtaking views from the top but also a paradise for hikers and outdoor enthusiasts.

Jotunheimen National Park:

Home to Norway's highest peaks, including Galdhøpiggen, Jotunheimen is a mecca for hikers. Glaciers, crystal-clear lakes, and vibrant flora define this national park.

Trolltunga:

Perched on the edge of a cliff, Trolltunga (Troll's Tongue) provides an adrenaline-pumping hiking experience and unparalleled panoramic views of the surrounding mountains.

Waterfalls: Nature's Symphony

Norway's waterfalls cascade down mountainsides, creating a mesmerizing symphony of sound and sight.

Vøringsfossen:

One of Norway's most famous waterfalls, Vøringsfossen plunges dramatically into the Måbødalen canyon, offering a spectacular viewing platform.

Kjosfossen:

Located along the Flåm Railway, Kjosfossen captivates with its sheer beauty, surrounded by lush greenery and accessible to railway passengers.

National Parks: Preserving Natural Treasures

Norway's commitment to preserving its natural wonders is evident in its national parks, where diverse ecosystems thrive.

Rondane National Park:

As Norway's first national park, Rondane is a high mountain plateau with rugged peaks, pristine lakes, and a habitat for reindeer and other wildlife.

Hardangervidda National Park:

The largest national park in Norway, Hardangervidda is a vast wilderness of plateaus, glaciers, and deep valleys, offering a haven for trekkers and nature lovers.

Outdoor Activities in Norway: Embrace the Thrill of Nature

Discover Norway's thrilling outdoor adventures, where the untouched landscapes serve as the backdrop for an array of activities that cater to both the adrenaline seeker and the nature enthusiast.

Hiking: Trails to Tranquility
Norway's vast network of hiking trails offers an exploration of its diverse terrain, from coastal paths to mountain summits.

Preikestolen (Pulpit Rock) Hike:
Overlooking the Lysefjord, the hike to Preikestolen rewards adventurers with a breathtaking plateau view. The trail winds through meadows and rocky terrain, promising an unforgettable experience.
Besseggen Ridge Hike:
For a panoramic view of two lakes separated by a dramatic ridge, the Besseggen hike in Jotunheimen National Park provides a challenging yet rewarding trek.

Skiing: Glide Through Winter's Wonderland
Norway's winter landscape transforms into a snowy wonderland, making it a haven for skiing enthusiasts.

Trysil:
As Norway's largest ski resort, Trysil offers a variety of slopes suitable for all levels. The crisp mountain air and powdery snow create an ideal setting for a memorable skiing experience.

Hemsedal:
Known as the Scandinavian Alps, Hemsedal provides a winter playground with vast ski areas and opportunities for cross-country skiing amid stunning vistas.

Kayaking: Paddle Through Pristine Waters
With its extensive coastline and network of fjords, Norway offers kayakers an unparalleled aquatic experience.

Nærøyfjord Kayaking:
Navigate the narrow channels of Nærøyfjord by kayak, immersing yourself in the tranquility of the surroundings while marveling at the towering cliffs.

Lofoten Islands Kayak Adventure:
Explore the crystal-clear waters around the Lofoten Islands, where dramatic peaks meet the sea. Kayak through secluded bays and embrace the serenity of the Arctic landscape.

Cycling: Pedal Through Scenic Routes
For those who prefer exploring on two wheels, Norway's cycling routes showcase its diverse landscapes.

Rallarvegen:
Ride along Rallarvegen, a historic cycling route that traverses mountains, valleys, and offers stunning views of glaciers, waterfalls, and lush meadows.

<u>Atlantic Ocean Road Cycling</u>:
Take on the challenge of cycling the Atlantic Ocean Road, an iconic route that combines exhilarating rides with breathtaking coastal scenery.

Embark on an adventure-filled journey through Norway's outdoor playground, where every trail, slope, and waterway beckons you to embrace the thrill of nature. Whether you seek the quietude of a hiking trail, the rush of downhill skiing, or the serenity of kayaking on tranquil fjords, Norway invites you to explore its pristine wilderness.

Norwegian Cuisine: A Culinary Expedition into Authentic Flavors

Dive into the heart of Norway's culinary landscape, where traditional dishes reflect the rich cultural tapestry of this Nordic nation. From savory delights to sweet indulgences, embark on a gastronomic journey that captures the essence of Norwegian cuisine.

Traditional Norwegian Dishes: Savory Delights

Rakfisk: Delight in the unique flavors of rakfisk, a traditional Norwegian fish dish. Consisting of fermented fish, typically trout or char, rakfisk is enjoyed with bread, potatoes, and sour cream.

Koldtbord: Experience the Norwegian smorgasbord known as koldtbord, featuring an array of cold dishes like cured meats, cheeses, pickled herring, and hearty bread. This communal feast is a celebration of local flavors.

Local Specialties: Culinary Gems of Norway

Lutefisk: Brave the taste of lutefisk, a dried fish dish soaked in a lye solution. Often served during festive occasions, lutefisk is accompanied by a medley of potatoes, peas, and bacon.

Pinnekjøtt: Savor pinnekjøtt, a Christmas specialty consisting of lamb ribs cured in a mixture of water, salt, and juniper berries. Slow-cooked to perfection, this dish is a holiday favorite.

Sweet Indulgences: Norwegian Desserts

<u>Krumkake</u>: Delight your taste buds with krumkake, a thin, crispy waffle cookie often filled with whipped cream. This sweet treat is a beloved part of Norwegian celebrations.

<u>Multekrem</u>: Indulge in multekrem, a luscious dessert featuring cloudberries mixed with sugar and whipped cream. This delightful concoction showcases the unique flavors of the Arctic.

Restaurant Recommendations: Culinary Hotspots

<u>Maaemo</u> (Oslo): Experience culinary excellence at Maaemo, a three-Michelin-starred restaurant in Oslo. Renowned for its focus on locally sourced ingredients, Maaemo offers a tasting menu that takes diners on a journey through Norwegian flavors.

<u>Bryggeloftet & Stuene</u> (Bergen): Immerse yourself in the historic ambiance of Bryggeloftet & Stuene in Bergen. This restaurant, located on the iconic Bryggen Wharf, serves traditional Norwegian dishes in a charming setting.

Tips for Trying Local Food: Embrace the Culinary Adventure

- Seek Local Markets: Explore local markets to discover fresh produce, artisanal cheeses, and handmade delicacies.
- Join Festivals: Attend food festivals to sample a variety of Norwegian dishes and engage with local chefs.
- Ask Locals for Recommendations: Connect with locals for insider tips on hidden culinary gems and must-try specialties.

Embark on a culinary adventure through Norway, where each dish tells a story of tradition, innovation, and the vibrant flavors that define this remarkable Nordic cuisine. From the simplicity of koldtbord to the intricate delights of Michelin-starred dining, Norway invites you to savor its culinary treasures.

Cultural Experiences: Unveiling Norway's Rich Heritage

Immerse yourself in the tapestry of Norwegian traditions and customs, where centuries-old practices blend seamlessly with contemporary celebrations. From vibrant festivals to cherished events, embark on a cultural journey that unveils the essence of Norway's rich heritage.

Norwegian Traditions: A Glimpse into the Past
Bunad Tradition:

Discover the beauty of the bunad, Norway's traditional folk costume. Each region boasts its unique bunad, reflecting intricate embroidery, vibrant colors, and historical significance. Embracing the bunad tradition is a testament to preserving Norway's cultural identity.

St. Olav Festival:

Partake in the St. Olav Festival, an annual celebration honoring St. Olav, Norway's patron saint. The festival features medieval reenactments, concerts, and processions, offering a captivating glimpse into the country's Christian heritage.

Festivals and Events: Celebrating the Norwegian Spirit
Midsummer Celebration:

Join the Midsummer celebration, a joyous occasion marking the summer solstice. Revel in traditional folk dances, bonfires, and the enchanting atmosphere as Norwegians welcome the longest day of the year.

Northern Lights Festival:
Experience the magic of the Northern Lights Festival, held in Tromsø. This cultural extravaganza showcases a blend of classical and contemporary performances, complemented by the mesmerizing backdrop of the Arctic sky.

Cultural Activities: Nurturing Artistic Expression
Viking Ship Museum:
Embark on a cultural voyage at the Viking Ship Museum in Oslo. Explore well-preserved Viking ships, artifacts, and exhibitions that shed light on Norway's seafaring history and the legendary Viking Age.

National Gallery (Nasjonalgalleriet):
Admire masterpieces at the National Gallery in Oslo, home to iconic Norwegian paintings, including Edvard Munch's "The Scream." This cultural hub provides insight into Norway's artistic legacy and its contribution to the global art scene.

Local Customs: Embracing Everyday Rituals
Coffee Culture:
Indulge in Norway's coffee culture, where the daily ritual of enjoying coffee and pastries, known as "kaffe og kaker," fosters social connections. Engage in leisurely conversations at local coffee shops, savoring the warmth of community and caffeine.

Hygge Lifestyle:
Embrace the hygge lifestyle, characterized by coziness, contentment, and a sense of well-being. Whether enjoying a fireside chat or relishing comfort food, Norwegians prioritize creating moments of hygge in their daily lives.

Tips for Cultural Exploration: Connect with Authenticity
1. Attend Local Gatherings: Participate in local gatherings, such as village festivals and community events, to witness authentic traditions.
2. Visit Open-Air Museums: Explore open-air museums like the Norsk Folkemuseum to experience historical dwellings, crafts, and demonstrations.
3. Learn Traditional Dances: Join in traditional folk dances during cultural events to engage with Norway's lively heritage.

Embark on a cultural odyssey through Norway, where time-honored traditions and contemporary celebrations harmonize to create a vibrant mosaic of cultural experiences. From the allure of bunads to the captivating festivities, Norway invites you to become part of its living heritage.

Historical Sites: Tracing Norway's Viking Legacy

Delve into the annals of time as we unveil the captivating historical sites that narrate the story of Norway's rich past, with a particular focus on its intriguing Viking history.

Viking Ship Museum (Vikingskipshuset), Oslo

Embark on a voyage through time at the Viking Ship Museum in Oslo. Marvel at remarkably preserved Viking longships, including the Oseberg, Gokstad, and Tune ships. These archaeological treasures provide a window into the seafaring prowess and craftsmanship of the Norse people during the Viking Age.

Bryggen Wharf, Bergen

Stroll through the UNESCO-listed Bryggen Wharf in Bergen, a testament to the city's Hanseatic trading past. Admire the colorful, iconic wooden buildings that once housed merchants and warehouses. Bryggen offers a glimpse into Bergen's medieval history and its role as a vital trading hub.

Nidaros Cathedral, Trondheim

Journey to Trondheim to behold the Nidaros Cathedral, a masterpiece of Gothic architecture. This majestic cathedral served as the coronation site for Norwegian monarchs and is a pilgrimage destination. Explore its intricate sculptures, stained glass windows, and the Nidaros Shrine, encapsulating centuries of religious and historical significance.

The Historical Museum (Historisk Museum), Oslo

Immerse yourself in Norwegian history at The Historical Museum in Oslo. From artifacts dating back to prehistoric times to exhibits on medieval Norway, the museum provides a comprehensive overview of the nation's evolution. Discover relics from the Viking era, shedding light on their daily lives, customs, and craftsmanship.

Urnes Stave Church, Luster

Visit the Urnes Stave Church, a UNESCO World Heritage site and the oldest stave church in Norway. Dating back to the 12th century, this medieval wooden church boasts intricate carvings and architectural splendor. Admire the fusion of Christian motifs with traditional Viking artistry, offering a glimpse into Norway's religious and cultural heritage.

Viking Village in Gudvangen

Step into a recreated Viking Village in Gudvangen, where history comes to life. Engage with costumed Viking reenactors, witness traditional crafts, and immerse yourself in the daily activities of the Norse people. Gain insights into their farming practices, domestic life, and the art of blacksmithing, providing a hands-on experience of Viking culture.

Insights into Norway's Viking Legacy:

1. Join Guided Tours: Opt for guided tours at historical sites for in-depth narratives on Viking history and the significance of each location.

2. Attend Viking Festivals: Plan your visit during Viking festivals, where historical reenactments and cultural events showcase the vibrancy of Norse traditions.

3. Explore Runestones: Seek out runestones, engraved with runic inscriptions, scattered across the country, offering glimpses into Viking communication and storytelling.

Embark on a historical odyssey through Norway's Viking legacy, where each site whispers tales of seafaring exploits, cultural exchange, and the enduring spirit of a remarkable era.

Transportation in Norway: Navigating the Land of Fjords

Embark on a seamless journey through Norway with this comprehensive guide to transportation, ensuring you explore the stunning landscapes and vibrant cities with ease.

Public Transportation: Trains, Buses, and Ferries

1. Trains:
Norway boasts an efficient and scenic train network. The Bergen Line and Flåm Railway offer breathtaking views. Consider the Norway in a Nutshell tour for a picturesque train journey.

2. Buses:
Intercity buses connect major cities and towns. Comfortable coaches traverse the scenic routes, providing an affordable and eco-friendly travel option.

3. Ferries:
With its extensive coastline and fjords, Norway relies on ferries. Experience a ferry ride through UNESCO-listed fjords like Nærøyfjord and Geirangerfjord.

Car Rentals: Driving Through Spectacular Landscapes
1. Renting a Car:
Enjoy the flexibility of exploring Norway's hidden gems by renting a car. Rental agencies are available at major airports and city centers.

2. Scenic Drives:
Navigate iconic routes like the Atlantic Road and Trollstigen. Witness awe-inspiring landscapes, picturesque villages, and cascading waterfalls.

3. Road Tolls:
Be aware of toll roads. Electronic toll collection is common; ensure your rental car is equipped with an AutoPASS device or pay online.

Domestic Flights: Connecting Cities and Regions
1. Domestic Air Travel:
Domestic flights link major cities like Oslo, Bergen, and Tromsø. Explore the convenience of air travel for covering longer distances.

2. Regional Airports:
Utilize regional airports for quick access to remote destinations. Small aircraft provide a unique perspective of Norway's diverse terrain.

3. Efficient Airports:

Norway's airports are known for efficiency and connectivity. Oslo Gardermoen Airport serves as the primary international gateway.

Navigating Transportation Systems: Insider Tips
1. Norway Pass:

Consider the Norway Pass for unlimited travel on trains and buses. Ideal for exploring multiple regions within a set timeframe.

2. Timely Planning:

Plan your itinerary with attention to transportation schedules. Timely connections ensure a smooth travel experience.

3. Fjord Cruises:

Explore fjords via organized cruises. These leisurely journeys offer a different perspective of Norway's coastal beauty.

Unlock the wonders of Norway by mastering its diverse transportation options. Whether you choose scenic train rides, embark on a road trip, or opt for domestic flights, Norway's transportation network seamlessly connects you to its unparalleled natural wonders and vibrant urban centers.

Accommodation Guide: Unveiling the Best Stays in Norway

Discover the perfect abode for your Norwegian adventure with our accommodation guide. From modern hotels to charming cabins, find the ideal lodging options to make your stay memorable.

Hotels: Modern Comfort Amidst Nature's Beauty

1. City Hotels:
In Oslo, Bergen, and other urban hubs, indulge in luxury and convenience at top-rated hotels. Enjoy world-class amenities and easy access to city attractions.

2. Fjord-Side Retreats:
Opt for hotels nestled along the fjords for unparalleled views. Wake up to the serene beauty of Norway's natural wonders right outside your window.

3. Northern Lights Hotels:
If chasing the Northern Lights is on your agenda, choose accommodations in Tromsø or Alta for optimal aurora viewing opportunities.

Hostels: Budget-Friendly and Social

1. Urban Hostels:
Experience Norway on a budget by staying in centrally located hostels. Connect with fellow travelers and explore the city's vibrant atmosphere.

2. Fjord-Side Hostels:
For a unique experience, stay in fjord-side hostels. Immerse yourself in nature while enjoying the camaraderie of like-minded adventurers.

3. Wilderness Hostels:
Venture into the wilderness and stay in remote hostels. Ideal for hikers and nature enthusiasts seeking an off-the-beaten-path experience.

Cabins: Embracing Tradition in Nature's Embrace

1. Traditional Cabins (Hyttas):
Immerse yourself in Norwegian culture by booking a traditional cabin. These hyttas offer a cozy retreat amidst stunning landscapes.

2. Mountain Cabins:

For avid hikers and skiers, mountain cabins provide a rustic yet comfortable shelter. Wake up surrounded by the majestic beauty of Norway's peaks.

3. Coastal Cabins:

Experience coastal living by renting cabins along the shores. Enjoy the sound of lapping waves and panoramic views of the sea.

Booking Tips: Securing Your Dream Stay

1. Early Reservations:

Secure popular accommodations by booking in advance, especially during peak seasons. Ensure availability and enjoy early-bird discounts.

2. Seasonal Considerations:

Tailor your stay based on the season. Choose fjord-side hotels for summer adventures and cozy cabins for winter retreats.

3. Local Experiences:

Opt for accommodations that offer local experiences. Stay in a fishing village cottage or a mountain cabin for an authentic taste of Norwegian life.

From urban elegance to rustic charm, Norway's diverse accommodations cater to every traveler's preference. Whether you seek the comforts of a city hotel or the tranquility of a fjord-side cabin, let your choice of stay enhance your Norwegian journey.

Seasonal Travel: Embracing Norway's Ever-Changing Beauty

Unveil the magic of Norway throughout the seasons, each offering a unique and breathtaking experience. Plan your visit wisely to capture the essence of this Nordic wonderland.

Spring: Blooms and Awakening Nature

Best Time to Visit: April to June
- Witness Norway come to life as vibrant blossoms blanket the landscapes.
- Explore botanical gardens, witness cascading waterfalls, and enjoy the charm of awakening cities.

Seasonal Activities:
- Fjord Cruises: Admire the blossoming fjord scenery under the gentle spring sun.
- Hiking Trails: Embark on nature trails surrounded by blooming wildflowers.
- Cultural Festivals: Participate in spring festivals celebrating music, art, and local traditions.

Summer: The Land of the Midnight Sun

Best Time to Visit: June to August
- Experience the enchanting phenomenon of the Midnight Sun, bathing the country in perpetual daylight.
- Enjoy extended daylight hours for exploration and outdoor adventures.

Seasonal Activities:
- Midnight Sun Tours: Take advantage of the extended daylight for hiking, biking, and sightseeing.
- Water Adventures: Kayak along serene fjords or cruise the crystalline waters.
- Outdoor Music Festivals: Attend lively music festivals held in various cities.

Autumn: A Symphony of Colors

Best Time to Visit: September to November
- Marvel at the kaleidoscope of autumn colors as forests transform into a visual masterpiece.
- Experience a more tranquil and less crowded Norway.

Seasonal Activities:
- Leaf Peeping: Drive through scenic routes or hike in national parks to witness the fall foliage.
- Northern Lights Preview: Catch the early glimpses of the Northern Lights as the nights grow longer.

Winter: A Snowy Fairy Tale

<u>Best Time to Visit: December to February</u>
- Immerse yourself in a winter wonderland with snow-covered landscapes.
- Ideal for winter sports enthusiasts and seekers of the Northern Lights.

<u>Seasonal Activities:</u>
- Skiing and Snowboarding: Hit the slopes in renowned ski resorts.
- Northern Lights Chasing: Venture to Tromsø or Alta for optimal Northern Lights viewing.
- Christmas Markets: Experience the magic of Norwegian Christmas markets.

Tailor your visit to Norway based on the season, each offering a distinctive charm. Whether it's the blossoms of spring, the endless daylight of summer, the vibrant hues of autumn, or the snowy landscapes of winter, Norway invites you to explore its diverse beauty year-round.

Cruise along the Norwegian Coast: Sailing with Hurtigruten

Embark on a maritime adventure with the renowned Norwegian Coastal Express, Hurtigruten. Explore the stunning coastline and picturesque ports that define Norway's maritime charm.

Hurtigruten: The Coastal Express Experience

Voyage of a Lifetime:
- Discover the world-renowned Hurtigruten, a daily passenger and freight shipping service.
- Immerse yourself in a coastal journey that seamlessly blends travel, exploration, and relaxation.

Scenic Coastal Route:
- Cruise along the majestic Norwegian coastline, witnessing breathtaking fjords, charming villages, and Arctic landscapes.
- Enjoy a perfect blend of comfort and coastal wonders, making every moment a postcard-worthy memory.

Ports of Call: Exploring Coastal Gems

1. Bergen: Gateway to the Fjords
- Start your journey in Bergen, a picturesque city surrounded by mountains and fjords.
- Explore the historic Bryggen Wharf and indulge in local cuisine.

2. Ålesund: Art Nouveau Delight

- Visit Ålesund, renowned for its Art Nouveau architecture.
- Stroll through its charming streets and climb to the Aksla Viewpoint for panoramic vistas.

3. Geiranger: Fjord Majesty

- Navigate through the iconic Geirangerfjord, a UNESCO World Heritage site.
- Witness stunning waterfalls, including the famous 7 Sisters.

4. Trondheim: Historical Riches

- Discover Trondheim's rich history, highlighted by the Nidaros Cathedral.
- Walk along the colorful wharves and experience the vibrant atmosphere.

5. Tromsø: Arctic Elegance

- Reach Tromsø, a city with a lively cultural scene and Arctic adventures.
- Visit the Arctic Cathedral and embark on Northern Lights excursions.

6. Kirkenes: Arctic Wilderness

Conclude your journey in Kirkenes, near the Russian border. Explore the Arctic wilderness and engage in unique winter activities.

Hurtigruten Tips: Navigating Your Coastal Adventure

1. Choose Your Season:

Experience the Midnight Sun in summer or the Northern Lights in winter.

2. Shore Excursions:

Opt for exciting shore excursions like dog sledding, fjord tours, and city exploration.

3. Onboard Comfort:

Enjoy comfortable cabins, delectable Norwegian cuisine, and panoramic lounges.

Embark on a coastal odyssey with Hurtigruten, where each port of call unveils a new chapter of Norway's maritime allure. Whether under the summer sun or winter's ethereal glow, this cruise promises an unforgettable exploration of Norway's coastal wonders.

Local Etiquette and Practical Tips: Navigating Norway with Grace

Cultural Etiquette: Embracing Norwegian Customs

1. Greetings:
A firm handshake is a common greeting. Maintain eye contact and use titles and last names until invited to use first names.

2. Punctuality:
Norwegians value punctuality. Arrive on time for appointments and social gatherings.

3. Tipping Culture:
Tipping is common but not obligatory. Round up the bill or leave a small percentage for good service.

4. Respect Personal Space:
Norwegians appreciate personal space. Avoid standing too close to others, especially with strangers.

5. Shoes Indoors:
It's customary to remove shoes when entering someone's home. Follow the host's lead.

6. Queueing:
Norwegians adhere to orderly queues. Wait your turn in lines and public spaces.

7. Alcohol Regulations:

Purchase alcohol in state-owned stores (Vinmonopolet). Drinking in public places is restricted.

8. Silent Public Transport:

Public transport is generally quiet. Keep conversations at a low volume and switch phones to silent mode.

9. Nature Respect:

Treat nature with respect. Avoid littering, stick to marked trails, and adhere to camping regulations.

10. Sustainable Practices:

- Norwegians prioritize sustainability. Join the effort by recycling, conserving energy, and using eco-friendly transportation.

Practical Tips: Enhancing Your Norwegian Adventure

1. Weather Readiness:
Pack layers and be prepared for changing weather, even in summer. Waterproof gear is essential.

2. Language Basics:
While many Norwegians speak English, learning a few basic Norwegian phrases is appreciated.

3. Currency and Payments:
Norway uses the Norwegian Krone (NOK). Credit cards are widely accepted, but it's wise to carry some cash in remote areas.

4. Transportation Efficiency:
Public transportation is efficient. Plan and book in advance for cost-effective travel.

5. Emergency Services:
Dial 112 for emergencies. Norway boasts excellent healthcare, but travel insurance is recommended.

6. Sunscreen in Summer:
In summer, the Midnight Sun can be intense. Pack sunscreen and sunglasses for outdoor activities.

7. Winter Driving Precautions:

If driving in winter, familiarize yourself with road conditions and use studded tires for snowy areas.

8. Opening Hours:

Shops often close early, especially on weekends. Plan shopping accordingly.

9. Wi-Fi Availability:

Stay connected with the widespread availability of Wi-Fi in hotels, restaurants, and public spaces.

10. Enjoy Local Cuisine:

- Sample traditional Norwegian dishes like rakfisk, lutefisk, and of course, fresh seafood.

Adhering to cultural etiquette and implementing practical tips ensures a seamless and respectful exploration of Norway. Embrace the customs, savor the landscapes, and create lasting memories in this enchanting Nordic realm.

Cool facts about Norway

Friluftsliv Fun in Norway! 🏔️

In Norway, they have a fantastic concept called "Friluftsliv," which is all about embracing the great outdoors! 🌲

Imagine being surrounded by rugged mountains, stunning snowscapes, dazzling auroras, and enchanting forests – Norway's got it all.
The Norwegians truly know how to appreciate the beauty of untouched nature, making outdoor adventures a vital part of their amazing way of life! 🏔️ 🌳

Napping Al Fresco! 😴 🍼

Prepare for cuteness overload! In Norway, it's totally normal for babies to catch their Z's outside. Yes, you read that right – actual babies, peacefully snoozing in their prams, while parents sip coffee or shop. 🛒

Why, you ask? It's not just for the adorable photo ops! This quirky tradition is believed to toughen up little ones against the elements. Safety first, though – Norway's got that covered, making it a cozy and safe naptime experience even at kindergartens! 🧣 👶

Sun's Embrace: Solveggen Magic! 🌼 😊

Behold the enchanting "Solveggen" – Norway's ode to the sun! 🌅

Imagine this: after enduring a lengthy winter, Norwegians eagerly await the first glimpse of sunlight. The moment a sunbeam peeks through, something magical happens. Locals flock outside, close their eyes, and bask in the warm embrace of the sun on their faces. 🌟

It's like a collective celebration of emerging from four months of near-complete darkness – a true Nordic phenomenon you'd happily join in! NO 🌟

Chill Vibes: Slow TV Extravaganza! 📺 NO

Get ready for a uniquely Norwegian TV experience – "Slow TV" or as they say, "sakte-TV"! 🚂

Imagine watching an entire seven-hour train journey without any edits or interruptions. Sounds wild, right? But in Norway, it's not just a TV genre; it's a stress-free, immersive way to enjoy the unhurried beauty of various processes. 🌿 📹

Curious? Give it a shot and let the Norwegian slow-paced magic captivate you! 🤩 ✨

Swedish Grocery Run: Norwegian Style! 🛒 SE

Living in Norway can be a bit pricey, and Norwegians have found a savvy solution – cross-border grocery shopping in Sweden! NO → SE

For those living close to the border, it's a strategic move. They embark on a quick round trip, snagging affordable groceries in Sweden to balance their budget. Ingenious, right? 🤑 ⚫

Skiing From Day One: Norwegian Style!

Ever heard the saying, "Norwegians are born with skis on their feet"? Well, it's not an exaggeration! 🧤🍼

From the moment they learn to walk, Norwegian kids are introduced to the thrill of skiing. 🏔️

With a history of Nordic ski use dating back over 5,000 years, it seems like a timeless tradition!
Even in urban areas, don't be surprised to spot locals gracefully skiing alongside their energetic four-legged companions. 🐾 ❄️

Early Birds at the Dinner Table!

Ever been to a place where dinner is served at 4 or 5 in the afternoon?

Welcome to Norway! NO Norwegians have a unique dining schedule, and dinner is fashionably early.

If you're planning a dinner invitation, better aim for the early side to avoid creating diplomatic tensions!

Shoes Off, Please! 👟 🚫

In Norway, homes are sacred, and entering with shoes on is a big no-no! 🚷

It's not just a preference; it's practically a rule.

Shoes stay at the door, ensuring cleanliness and a bit of Norwegian home etiquette! NO ✨

Double Talk! 🗣️NO

Norwegian language, a linguistic tale of two! 📜NO Bokmål, rooted in historical ties with Denmark, and Nynorsk, a 19th-century creation from various local dialects. 🗣️📚

Embracing diversity, Norway keeps its linguistic heritage alive!

Winter Wheels! ❄️ 🚲

Norwegians pedal through snow and frost with a smile! 😃 🚴

In Norway, bikes brave the chill, adorned with big wheels and spiked tires, while bikers bundle up. 🧤 ❄️

No bad weather, just bad clothes – they spin through winter, eco-friendly and outdoorsy!

Experiences You Need to Have in Norway

1.) Ride The Flåm Railway

Arguably one of the prettiest train journeys in the world, the Flåmsbana is a 12 mile train journey in the magical and pristine landscape of Aurland in Norway. You can arrive in Bergen or Oslo and take the train from Myrdal directly to the stunning fjord lined town of Flåm that will leave you breathless. There are multiple trains going back and forth so this can make for the perfect day trip!

As the train climbs over 800 metres, you will be transported into a whole new world (seriously – the landscape transforms from snow capped mountains as far as the eye can see to dramatic lush greenery in minutes)! It really is even more stunning than you can imagine and we can't recommend it enough.

2.) Explore Stavanger

Stavanger is one of Norway's largest cities and it's a great place to start your Nordic adventure, with an airport that's connected to many European destinations. This city is a perfect way to experience Nordic life albeit in a more intimate setting that say the capital, Oslo. It's also got lots of fantastic little cafes and bars where you can easily spend far too many hours sipping of alcoholic (or otherwise) libations...

3.) Get The Best View Of Norway's Largest & Most Famous Fjord From Stegastein Lookout

Sognefjord is also the 2nd largest fjord in the world and home to the UNESCO World Heritage site of Naeroyfjord. A 20 minute drive from Flåm, Stegastein Lookout is the perfect place to visit on a Norwegian sunny day. When the weather is clear you can see for miles, right through the dramatic and winding fjords that cover this beautiful region.

4.) Discover Bergen's Secret Forest

Okay, it's not so secret but a little elusive if you're as lazy as I am. See, the forest is tucked in Fløyen which is the hill where you can get the best view of the city which involves a pretty decent hike. Thankfully, there's also a funicular (a train of sorts) that takes you right up to the top so you can skip the hike.

5.) ...While You're Up In Floyen, Watch The Sunset Over Bergen

No trip to Bergen is complete without experiencing the warm hues of a Nordic sunset. It's a breathtaking view that's only made better by packing a warm drink (for winter) or a good old Nordic brew in summer.

6.) Fish For Your Supper In The North Sea

While in the Stavanger region, why not try your hand at fishing? It's a great way to see a new perspective of the Nordic coast... even if your fishing skills are as terrible as mine. I went to bed hungry that night! (Or I would have if I didn't raid the restaurant in our hotel!)

7.) Climb The Epic Pulpit Rock

A real feat for any traveller, climbing pulpit rock is one of those 'must-do' things in Norway. Taking around 6 hours (there and back – less if you're a seasoned hiker) this climb is best tackled on a dry day with lots of water and sugary snacks. The hike can be a little tough at times (albeit VERY doable, even if you're inexperienced and wearing the wrong shoes like we did) but rest assured your wobbly legs will forgive you once you see view from the top! It's definitely an unforgettable experience and one that you will brag about for quite a long time afterwards.

8.) Discover The UNESCO World Heritage Site of Bryggen In Bergen

Right by the eastern side of the fjords in Bergen is the historic UNESCO old town area of the city, Bryggen. This beautifully preserved wooden houses and alleyways are a great place to spend a few hours exploring the heritage of the city. Take the opportunity to pop into one of the many beautiful restaurants within the buildings themselves.

9.) Go Thrill Seeking With A Fjord Safari

One of the best ways to explore the fjords themselves are by boat, obviously! For an experience like no other take a fjord safari from Flåm where you will be whisked off through the dramatic fjords that weave through this beautiful region. There is a real benefit on going on a much smaller and faster boat too, you can get up close and personal with many aspects of the fjords... seeing the seals, whales and even getting sprayed by the glacial waterfalls that stream down into the water... brrrrrr!

For More Fun and Interesting Facts Books,
Please visit our author page
"Aicha Safari"

Printed in Great Britain
by Amazon

38366977R00044